VOICES OF ANCIENT EGYPT

BY KAY WINTERS

ILLUSTRATED BY

BARRY MOSER

NATIONAL GEOGRAPHIC

WASHINGTON, D. C.

To Marta Felber, who introduced me to Egypt —KW

For Kay —BM

The author, illustrator, and publisher would like to thank
Edward Bleiberg, Associate Curator, Egyptian, Classical,
and Ancient Middle Eastern Art, Brooklyn Museum of Art,
for carefully reviewing both text and illustrations for historical
accuracy and for supplying us with the proper
hieroglyphics for the titles.

Text copyright © 2003 Kay Winters
Illustrations copyright © 2003 Barry Moser
First paperback printing 2008
Paperback ISBN: 978-1-4263-0400-2

The illustrations in this book are watercolor on paper.
Book design by Bea Jackson.
The text of the book is set in Gilgamesh.

Library of Congress Cataloging-in-Publication Data

Winters, Kay.
Echoes of ancient Egypt / by Kay Winters ; illustrated by Barry Moser.
    p. cm.
Summary: Individual craftsmen, artists, and laborers describe the work
that they do in Egypt during the time of the Old Kingdom, and the
historical note places them in context.
ISBN 0-7922-7560-8 (hard cover)
1. Egypt—Civilization—To 332 B.C.—Juvenile literature. 2.
Occupations—Egypt—Juvenile literature. [1. Egypt—Civilization—To 332
B.C. 2. Occupations—Egypt.] I. Moser, Barry, ill. II. Title.
DT61 .W58 2003
932—dc21

                                    2001007356

Founded in 1888, the National
Geographic Society is one of the largest
nonprofit scientific and educational
organizations in the world. It reaches
more than 285 million people worldwide
each month through its official journal,
NATIONAL GEOGRAPHIC, and its four other magazines; the National
Geographic Channel; television documentaries; radio
programs; films; books; videos and DVDs; maps; and
interactive media. National Geographic has funded more
than 8,000 scientific reasearch projects and supports an
education program combating geographic illiteracy.

NATIONAL GEOGRAPHIC SOCIETY
1145 17th Street N.W.
Washington, D.C. 20036-4688 U.S.A.
Visit the Society's Web site: www.nationalgeographic.com

PRINTED IN MEXICO

CONTENTS

About the Hieroglyphics

The titles in this book are printed in two languages—English and ancient Egyptian (hieroglyphics). The ancient Egyptian translations come from the *Concise Dictionary of Middle Egyptian* by R. O. Faulkner.

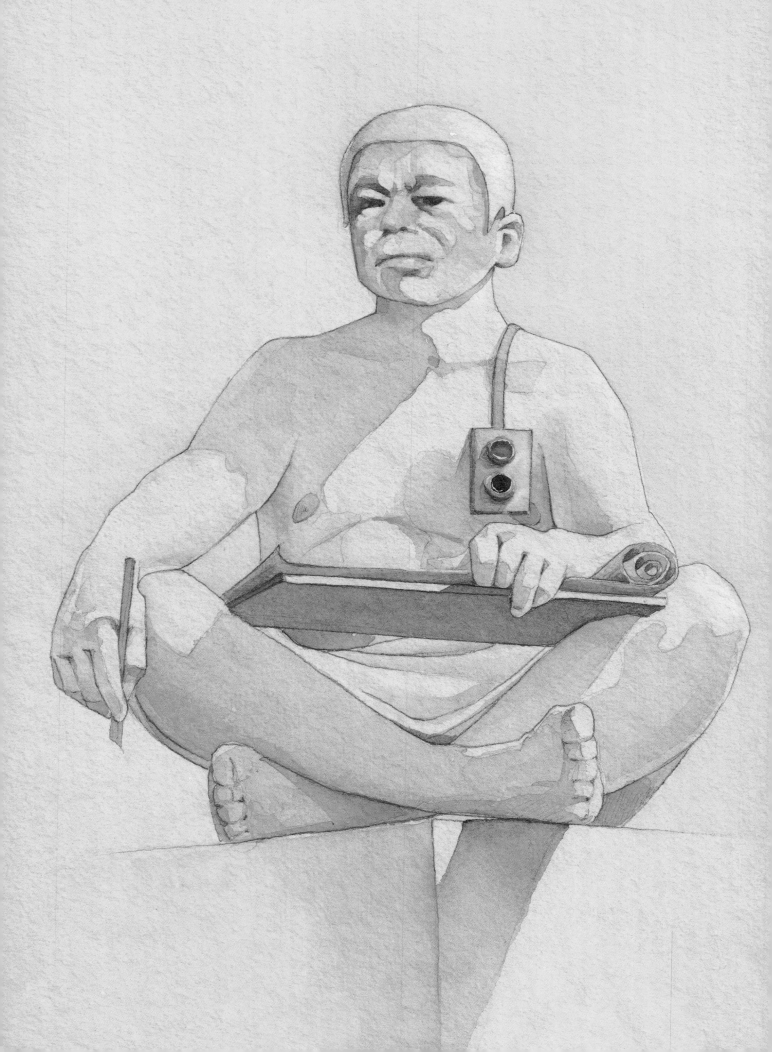

The Scribe

I study day and night,

learn law, literature, and mathematics,

copy retold tales.

I am my father's dream,

daring to be more than he.

While others bear lashes to build tombs,

dodge crocodiles to fish the Nile,

weave cloth in airless rooms,

I unlock secrets in ancient scrolls,

weave wisdom from times gone by.

In a kilt of white, I measure the Nile,

count the cattle, register the harvest.

No taxes on my goods!

Because of me, voices of the village come alive.

Hear my people speak.

With reed brush and cake of ink

I record our days.

The Farmer

My husband and I work the master's land.

After floods rise, we guide water into narrow lanes,

drenching dusty clay.

Weeks pass while water soaks the earth.

Time for the sowing of the seed.

The driver urges the oxen with a stick.

My husband pushes plough handles down deep.

The driver cries, "Pull hard." He prods the team.

I follow behind, breaking clods of soil

with my wooden hoe.

We scatter seed. Sheep trod and trample.

Seeds sink and settle into black mud.

Now is the time for waiting

for those first small shoots.

Now is the time for watching

for worms, mice, locusts, the hippopotamus.

All are enemies of the sower of seed.

At the harvest the scribe measures the grain.

The master is pleased.

We give thanks to the god Min, friend of the farmer.

We bow to barley, sing to the Nile.

Together we have worked the land.

The Pyramid Builder

The Nile is flooding. It's time!

Like thousands of my countrymen,

I leave my village and go to Giza to serve Pharaoh,

to carve his stairway to the sky.

I am a cutter of stone as well as a planter of seed.

Barges bring yellow limestone from dusty quarries.

Side by side with other stonecutters,

I lift my mallet, pound the chisel.

We size the stone, level the high spots,

square the two-ton block.

Haulers slide the stone on a sled.

Water bearers run ahead to soak the mud,

which coats the rising ramp.

Masons push the block into place.

A scribe keeps count.

Year after year, in sun that scalds, we toil for Pharaoh.

He gives us radishes, onions, bread to eat,

a place to sleep.

Each day I pray the gods will not let the stone I work

roll back and crush me into dust.

But I am proud to help shape the House of Eternity.

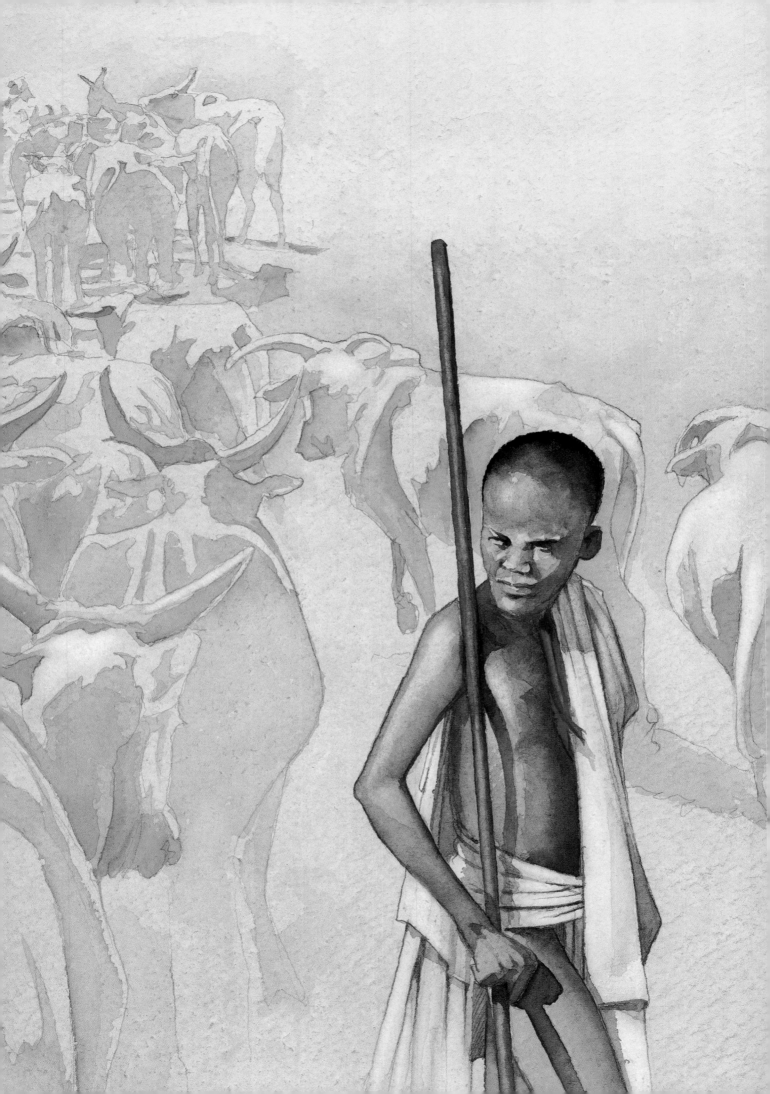

The Herdsman

The cattle are my children.

With soft words, I spend my days

tending, feeding, birthing.

I fatten cows with rolls from boiled dough.

In summer, we herdsmen travel north

where our cattle graze in grassy fields.

We live in reed huts, roast ducks upon the fire,

tell tall tales, and guard our herds.

Heading home, we wade the river's branch,

watchful for the crocodile.

I carry the smallest calf upon my back.

Now cattle, fat and sleek, await counting

by the scribe.

I am the herdsman,

the cows, my kin.

The Birdnetter

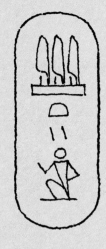

Look up! Look above!

The cranes, the doves, the ducks are coming.

I am the snarer of birds.

How fortunate I am to work in open air,

in green fields and leafy marshes.

Bright winged waterbirds, pigeons, and quail

swarm over Egypt.

My nets and traps are ready.

I trap geese then fatten them with dough,

just as the herdsman feeds his cattle.

Plump and tasty,

these birds could grace the Pharaoh's table

and sometimes do.

I water the crane, with his slim stilt neck,

a pretty present for the master's daughter.

My family and I do not go hungry,

for the sky is loud

with the beating of wings.

I am the birdnetter.

I wonder how it would feel

to fly?

The Washer of Clothes

I am a washer of clothes.

Brother to the crocodile,

I spend my days in water.

I soak the clothes, beat them with a wooden stave,

then wrap them around a stick

to wring out the wet.

White linen soils quickly in our hot dry land.

I scrub goose grease, wine stains, the juice of berries.

I deliver clean kilts, skirts, cloaks, and robes

to my master's household.

To be clean of body,

dressed in spotless garb

is the mark of those I serve.

The Nile is my workplace.

I know no other.

The Weaver

Weaving is women's work.

Ancient tales tell that goddesses

spun and wove the clothes of Osiris.

I follow in their sandal prints,

making linen smooth as silk.

The flax is boiled, beaten with hammers,

cleaned by hand.

The spinner chooses fibers to form her thread,

then twists and turns her spindles.

I work the warp and woof with the shuttle

on a horizontal loom.

Though days are long and the room is close,

my cloth shimmers in the sunlight.

It is packed unfolded into boxes

and carried off on poles

to the royal House of Silver.

My own garments may be coarse,

my husband just a peasant,

but I create cloth fit for gods.

The Goldsmith

My gold comes from Nubia,

where captives live in stone huts

and mine the vein.

I know the secret ways of working gold,

how to twist wires, cut strips, set stones.

I make jewelry for the living and the dead.

My circlets gleamed

on the arm of the Queen

as she rode down the Nile.

When she passed on

to the Land That Loves Silence,

those bracelets were tucked in her tomb.

I am the goldsmith.

My work glitters almost as bright as our sun god Re.

Village heads turn when I walk by.

The Embalmer

"Come at once," the servant begs.

"My master is dead."

He is asking me, chief priest,

to perform the sacred rites.

Back at my workshop, I wash the body,

while another priest murmurs incantations.

My flint knife makes the first incision.

I take the stomach, lungs, intestines, liver

and store them in canopic jars.

I leave the heart, home of the spirit,

but pull the brains out with a hook of bronze.

We dry the body with crystals of natron.

Forty days pass.

We wind the head, the chest, the trunk, the limbs

with yards of linen.

On the eighty-ninth day

we place him in the cedar coffin.

Secretly, I believe the chief priests

are more important than Pharaoh.

No spirit can rise skyward without our sacred touch.

The Dancer

My troupe moves in and out as one,
no feast complete without our presence.

We dance to praise,
give thanks for the rising of the Nile,
the harvest gathered in.
We stretch and bend,
mirror one another in stately style.
We click our clappers.
The singers follow close behind.

We dance to mourn.
At the Feast of Eternity
we usher the spirit on his journey.
We celebrate the one who's gone
to the Field of Peace.
His statue watches.
Even when they are sorrowing,
we delight the guests.
I am a dancer.
My job is joy.

The Carpenter

The Pharaoh sends his carpenters to Lebanon

in search of cedar to build his barge.

I go with fellow shipwrights to the land of trees.

Wood is scarce in Egypt,

except the lowly sycamore,

too knotty to suit our careful craft.

We axe the trunks, cut the cedar planks,

and haul them home.

I use my adze, mallet, chisel, and saw

to shape the wood.

At last the ship is ready to set sail.

The Great One comes

and boards his barge.

He is well pleased.

I stand on shore and watch my weeks of work

afloat.

The Sailor

When I hoist the sails

like white wings of cranes,

off we go.

But when the wind weakens,

rowers dip and pull.

We sail south on the Red Sea

until the land of strangers can be seen.

After we dock, we lay out gifts—

beads, daggers, bread, meat, and fruit—

for the goddess Hathor.

Days pass while we fill our hold

with tribute for Egypt—

ebony, ivory, trees of myrrh,

and monkeys who climb and swing from the mast.

At last we travel home,

a ship of treasure from the place of Punt.

And I, a sailor, have been beyond.

The gods willing, I will go again.